Wake Up and Dream

Michael Rothenberg

MadHat Press
Asheville, North Carolina

MadHat Press
MadHat Incorporated
PO Box 8364, Asheville, NC 28814

Copyright © 2017 Michael Rothenberg
All rights reserved

The Library of Congress has assigned
this edition a Control Number of
2017937422

ISBN 978-1-941196-48-9 (paperback)

Cover art by Marc Vincenz
Cover design by Terri Carrion and Marc Vincenz
Book design by MadHat Press

www.MadHat-Press.com

First Printing

to Joanne Kyger and Terri Carrion

Table of Contents

Tropical Alley	1
You're Broke, On Drugs, and Monsanto Owns You	2
Skinhead	4
Terroristic	6
The Vanities	8
The Blue Jays	11
The March	13
Independence Day	21
Ribbons	22
Serenity Spring	26
Where Are the Saints Buried?	30
Rome	31
Revolt of the Donkeys	33
Remembering *The Majoon Traveler*	41
Plus C'est La Même Chose Agadir	45
Platform 18, Milano Centrale	46
Bozo the Slick	49
Miracle Pastry	55
No Grandi Navi	58
Wooden Ducks	63
When I Was in Italy	64
The Portal	71
Wake Up and Dream	73
Acknowledgments	88
About the Author	89

Tropical Alley

A black man struggles
    with a black umbrella blown
        inside out

    Rain falls
        one drop at a time

A white man
    in a purple driver's cap
        sleeps

    in a corroded
        aluminum chair.

January 22, 2014

Michael Rothenberg

You're Broke, On Drugs, and Monsanto Owns You

So what are ya gonna do about it?
All those young people attached to their teeth

    Screams in an empty house
    Sanity of suicide at daybreak

        Thank god the dogs woke me up

I wander out into imagination's junkyard
Strewn with electronic demons
Screeching and tugging at love
And at the end of the day
The windmills lose the war

        It's clear we don't need
      Those twinkly lights on the Bay Bridge
           Even though they call it ART

    Pity those sweet white kids
    Their middle class frustrations
    Under-loved, over-drugged
    They never read books, instead
    They resurrect zombies in the suburbs
    I tell them without shame

I am a madman
A gardener
An effete capitalist
I want a chocolate bunny
Wisteria makes me happy

        What can I do about it?
        I need a million dollars to feed
        A lot of hungry babies

What can I do about it?
In my own backyard everyday
A separate peace
But I never let the poetic melody lead me

        The dog wants my chair
        Someone in the back of my head says,
        "Give it to him"
        But I don't

One week later
I'm stealing poems from an undergrad student
That's all I can do about it.

                                  April 23, 2013

Michael Rothenberg

Skinhead

This planet needs more martyrs
Yay martyrs!
Sacrificed on the Altar of the Holy Beast
For the sake of the Holy Dream!

Everybody knows
Poets have a right to say
Whatever they want to say
And so sometimes they say it without shame
When they're free….

Poets, those hoarders!
Hoarders without borders!
We have surrendered
Our craft to the totalitarian regime
We were so very smart, naïve
Confident and lazy
So unimaginative!
We just handed over the key

Now the government
Requires unrestricted access to all
Colonoscopy cameras
If you have nothing to hide it won't be a problem
"Relax your sphincters, patriots!
Here comes the peggin' president!"

But wait, there's hope
Today, the windmills were defeated
Good news!
We're finally getting somewhere.

July 13, 2013

Michael Rothenberg

Terroristic

Downstream from the incinerated calamity
Wheat rises from a bone-yard exodus

    Sunset at Taiji Cove
    Satin monoxide corridors

        "I can't breathe!"

Migration of the armored cemetery
The ancient howling latitudes
Honey-shackled sunsets

    The pink eclipse at 4 a.m.

        Corrosive linguistic fakery
        Leaves spun on a static loom
        Ducklings in a petroleum eddy

Bellows wheeze in purple swollen light
Toxic figurines waltz over swollen graves
Swans of fire sail on a dying synapse

    Under the boughs of a blood division
    Hungry blades scorch the velvet harness

      Shit springs up from the ground
      Lithium worms wriggle through the clouds
      The skin of the gleaner's hands and feet
      Crack in the faint sun

Wisteria petals spill lavender on the pebble path
Hummingbirds roar through the radioactive forest
Beheadings and amputations float
In the coral shallows

      Insects click in the coiled iron prism of a nightmare
      Sticks gather in a furious bundle
      Beneath the broken willow

To tremble in the slaughter
To swim in atom light
To turn forever on a sleepless swell.

January 10, 2015

Michael Rothenberg

The Vanities

       I saw the last
great elephant

      fall to the ground,
  slaughtered

     for her tusks

Epic memories
forgotten

in Phoenix, Arizona

I saw a hat
made from feathers

of an extinct
Amazonian bird

     the day
     beauty perished

  in whispers

Victims

        of an ordinary
        world

in Demming,
New Mexico

        I heard a child
        scream

A child I know

        Startled awake

in the middle
of the black and blue night

The diminishing voice

of justice
        in Blythe, California

Destination Florida

        I saw highways

Michael Rothenberg

named after wars
    and dead heroes

Crosses
  on the side of the road

       Everywhere

  in the USA

causeways
rise and fall

    to apocalypse.

The Blue Jays

The Chinese horses march across the wall again
A quiet biography of leaves
The war continues

> Books
> A collection of sufferings
> I don't want to see them anymore

Take me back to the blue jays
To the squirrels munching in the redwoods
The dogs and Terri and I

> My son, on a better day, full of wonder at Saturn
> On New Year's Eve in the Everglades
> An alligator!

Take me back to the blue jays
Nature noises. Open beams
Tongue in groove

> But I miss my friends in Italy
> "Come back!" she says
> I'd like to do that now, I say, but the blue jays,
> somebody has to look after the blue jays
> while I'm away....

Michael Rothenberg

Take me back to the blue jays
To another time and place

>When I was angry and had something to say
>When the Buddha lived on the deck at night
>and incense brought me home.

The March

The angry man
Tired man

Blue-feathered squawking
Man. One million miles
From love

        Symphonic transgressions
        Scorch the withering ozone

*

Under topless limelight
The colorless wave crashes
        Against the mossy foot of the puffy green lawn chair

                In the tree house

        Herbal licorice twists on Sundays
        Corncobs glow in fractured disco party forest chatter

                "Fuck you. Fuck you very, very much"

Aggression builds a toothpick fortress

*

Michael Rothenberg

      Perseid meteor shower

Wireless elephants on electronic Serengeti
Trumpet to a deity they can trust

Raise the brass for freedom
In the great, golden wildebeest migration

          … awakening microbes on a dark
      and cherry blossom planet …

          *

The moose wades in the swamp, eats the water lilies
The rattlesnake eats the mouse headfirst
The black hole swallows a star

        I have never met a deity I could trust

    Fuck people!

        March on!

        *

    Lay down your arms beneath the smart old tree.…

Hundreds with a bullet to the head while some naïve …

The naked enemy, face in the dirt, children

  Some teetering dove shackled between laurels
  Coos for peace

    Fuck you!
    What does this prove?
    Fuck them!

  Who are they?
  They decide and we comply
  Or else we do nothing at all

    Still we march

    *

Lazy abusers making lists
Hand out condolences, apologies

A bait and switch offering of resurrection lilies
Boots on the ground, no boots, boots

  Purple stippling on that sideways screw

Michael Rothenberg

Each word I speak to my life is an affirmation
Each word a step or low lying down
An action

        Confirmation, communion, defiance

Each step I take is a determination of justice

        What do you do in the morning, first thing?
        Greet the day?
        Or bitch and scream at the brutality of night?
        The robbery of an ill-conceived day gone by?

        *

    Political rectitude, collateral damage

Hold on, it's coming, you will know justice soon enough!
Here comes another bruise

        Morning marches on....

        *

Gun manufacturers, gunrunners, police and soldiers
The boys in blue with toys, in green and brown in blood

The narrative of apocalypse everywhere
People either accept it or reject it
If they accept it there will be hell to pay
If they reject it they will do some good in the world

(We make plans for a war in Syria)

We make plans for a Mars invasion
Introduce ourselves forcibly
Upon distant and peaceful microbes
If we are successful we can put them to work for us
Good slaves make good neighbors!

*

Shorter, concise, ordinary
An extraction, twig in a puddle, extraordinary, uranium

Anaerobic, alluvial, swag
Bling, phosphorous bling

An allocation of resources, a buzzword bangle
Sacrament, woodpecker, balcony

Procession, pulse, flow, ring of bones

Michael Rothenberg

108, 109, 212, 550
Lucky 13 and magic 3, illusive 7

*

The issue, substance
Denouncement, celebration, flux

Pillory, noose, helix, daisy chain, subsequent quandary
Debilitation, simulacra, compost, flarb

Quietude, beatitude, amplitude, brocade
The bothering, othering, slough

    Dice, water glass, glass of water, celadon teacup
    Spice rack

        Count them!
        The bombs!

          Twice the door is opened
          Three times the door is closed

I didn't hear it the first time

*

The march continues toward the revelatory unknown

*

Slow things creep out of the new place
    towards glabrescent green restitution

        Simplex

. . .

        Green Corn Moon

King Lear in old growth forest amphitheater
Orates cannabinoid intoxication cures
For an early morning wake-up call

    Those stones offshore in the silver calm

        An oceanic Zen garden, the concentric swells
        Ripples vanish in the duality of a foggy sky

"You *fence* it in" or maybe you don't

*

Michael Rothenberg

My father went to sleep one night
And never awoke
He travels with a water moccasin
Through the brackish canals of paradise
While pots and pans bang in the windows of Bogota

    Where the revolution begins …

In an alabaster foyer
Dappled with white gardenia, air-conditioned samovars
And strawberries
A scarlet cat purrs on a pillow beside
My recently departed mother

    The Queen of Cats!

    *

    I can almost hear them shout
    I can almost hear them scream.

    August 10, 2013–December 2016

Independence Day

Do you ever feel like a slave?
Or want to be President of The World?

Is there a conspiracy of silence?
Or is humanity finally standing up to the oppressor?

O, how those poor and huddled masses
Struggle against unyielding forces

The mind imagines a universe!
Great people of the world awake

In the fierce shadow of the marketplace
We are on our way up!

August, 2013–July 4, 2014

Michael Rothenberg

Ribbons

When I see ribbons in winter morning light
I know I haven't slept long enough

Seated at the kitchen table in the tropical cottage
Cup of Cuban coffee in my hand

Weary of the human condition
Notes will not be enough

Ribbons scream....

*

Hollywood, Florida
Three o'clock in the afternoon

Blue light streaks through
Frosted jalousie windows

The dog sleeps, wakes, listens
Looks, barks, sleeps

I am lying in gloom
Suffering from a condition

Throbbing brow, aching eyes
There's no one here to set me free

*

Terri visits her mother down the street
She can't manage me any longer

She wants me to take a terrible walk
With the dogs but I don't want to go

Anywhere. I want to drift through
The shadowy bedroom ether

Of this Florida afternoon. Numb
Myself with wine and pills, imagine

Baudelaire (borderlands) and Henry Miller
Exhausted senses, wild visions

Timelessness, days without dates
(Deities) or meaning. Afternoons

without purpose (Affirmations)
I want to drown in the quicksand

Michael Rothenberg

Of sensuality with nothing to win
Nothing to gain and no one to torture

*

So I'm going home now
Dialing the phone number of the house

I once lived in 50 years ago
It rings through to an electronic nowhere land

Going nowhere. Just ringing, ringing
Back to my mother's voice

Or in this case to the housekeeper
"Rothenbergs' residence"

Is my mother there, Ophelia?
"No Michael, she's not home anymore"

Again, every once in a while when I panic
I can't help but reach for the telephone

I find myself calling my childhood home
Ringing, ringing, to nowhere

"There is no connection"
I figured that out one drunken night in 1984

(Wrapped in fog). No matter where I am
There is no connection.

January 7, 2014

Michael Rothenberg

Serenity Spring

One day the story changed
And those people who want to help out

They're incompetent. All of them!
Breeding little dogs to carry around

In a purse. A conspiracy of blue jays
Indecipherable spider webs

Surveillance in every corner of the forest
You can only imagine

What the clouds say
Suspicious signals from the sun

A revolt of hurricanes!

*

"What have we done to the earth?"

>For years Industry told us
>About "Better living through chemistry"
>
>And now that we don't like what Industry
>does we pretend they never said it

Listen to squirrel chatter
Militant moles message underground

Agitate the atmosphere
Until there's nothing left of hope

    (Only holes and shelled nuts)

    Fracking, fracking, fracking, cracking

The Great American Optimism!
Corporate Venture Cyclops!

    *

    There is no peace
    The Buddha

    Buried
    Buried and unearthed

    Buried and unearthed
    Ashes to ashes

    Vanity to vanity

Michael Rothenberg

Greetings Serenity!

*

I spoke to myself on the deck last night
We reconciled beneath the stars

Waltzed to a raccoon love song
While all the fools in paradise watched

Today the silent sun grows
And burns and burns

I remember pink towels on the garden chair
My mother's cool gardenia hand

On my fevered head. A difficult breath
Still hidden in the leaves....

*

There are two worlds I know
The one I run from and the one I hold on to

For dear life. I don't own either
Beware of the purple doppelganger!

Serenity loiters in fern hollow....
So I watch the red geraniums grow

And help them along the best I can
Sweet Serenity Spring.

January 2014

Michael Rothenberg

Where Are the Saints Buried?

I lock the door
three times because

I can't remember
what I used to know

Now tell me quick
Where are the saints buried?

Rome

Nemo propheta in patria sua

        The boy opened the road

        Unified body and soul

            With poetry in Lampedusa

The boy saw the temporal

Passage to conclusion

        In pop culture and the fall of idols

Hysteria's Continent, lament

The angry human race

Blue multitudes

            Pristine archives

            Tabula rasa redux

Michael Rothenberg

                                              The tall magic lantern

An Oedipal dream of tangerine genies

Effervescent blush upon a star

The boy in the shadows.

                                                            May 1, 2014

Revolt of the Donkeys

for Noureddine Bazine, May 2014

Only fools
plan

for a better
world

Five minutes
a day

under
the carob tree

we speak
without

fetters
But mostly

we carry
carts

of sweet
oranges

Michael Rothenberg

to the market
Lean

against
the heat

and blood-
fissured

fortress wall
and weep

for our
masters

Not so much
for ourselves

The road
is long

and awkward
We stop

at the gasoline
station

for rice
and olive salad

The water
comes

from the cooler....
Meanwhile

the American
donkey

tosses
in the back seat

and thinks of
an air-conditioned

nightmare
Which raises

the price of travel
Making

life
more difficult

Michael Rothenberg

for a donkey
on a third

world income
But

for scholars
who need

to be cool,
we pay

the price
and continue

our journey
east

While
Africa

weeps
While

Mexico,
Macedonia,

Egypt,
Tunisia,

Libya
Syria

and
some

very
specific

regions
of the USA

weep
Actually,

we bray
not weep

Grunt
not weep

Everywhere
permaculturists

Michael Rothenberg

and
counterculturists

Even
journalists

like you,
Nourredine,

who write
for the culture

section
of the national

news,
bray!

I will never
understand

why
we don't

give up
our revolt

and pay
attention

to the authorities
who know

best how to
manage

our fragile
resources

Still,
together

we weep
Bray

and weep
Like

Um Rabi'a
River

which lately
has been

Michael Rothenberg

running
dry

Oh,
poor donkey,

save
your tears!

There's
nothing

we can do
about it

The Chinese
are coming

soon
to build

the future
and

donkey
meat is cheap.

Remembering *The Majoon Traveler*

Exotic poverty
and public

drunkenness
Souls

that climb
like the Atlas

Mountains
Going up

and down
freely

by themselves
We never

talk about
the gluttony

of kings
Dyed

in the wool
in the old way

Michael Rothenberg

There are no
books

for modern
intellectuals

Travel abroad
is difficult

And men
still go

hand in hand
on

uneven streets
and beach

promenade
Like the old days

they bring
mint tea

in tall glasses,
steeped

in sugar and sky
That's what

Habib told us
He says

he will take us
there

to some forgotten
butterfly

long before
the death

of Gabriel García
Márquez

Or the birth
of Mohammed

Mrabet
When honey

stuck
in the teeth

Michael Rothenberg

of the astral
shepherd

and the spotted
goat

climbed
the argan tree

to the realm
of Jilala

and the sleepless
beggar.

Plus C'est la Même Chose Agadir

Simmering tagine
Eel and peppers

      Braying donkeys and alley cats
      Doves gathered at the gates of the souk

          Amber resin beads and lapis lazuli
          The saffron glow of Moroccan leather

No, I haven't heard the muezzin
Call us to our knees

      But there's a snake charmer to charm us
      And a poet to take us wherever we want to go

          And what about change? I ask.
          There must be change!

"Do not worry about change," Habib says.
"Change will take care of itself."

May 4, 2014

Michael Rothenberg

Platform 18, Milano Centrale

When the idea of holocaust
becomes more potent

than The Holocaust itself
When "indifference" is conceptual

And in quotes
And you spend 10 million dollars to remember....

And you still can't remember
The train bangs down the tracks

                *

Graffiti
The Grand Design of Mafia/government

Boondoggles
Villages of War trapped in time

Which war?
Which man-made circle of hell?

Captured by a philosophy

      Achoo!

*

Sweat and fire
Piercing contractions

Suspended in an invisible frame
Daylight of prominent crucifixion

*

I've been to the most secret place

*

The black and white cows will never come home
A pigeon rides a lion frozen in the Duomo

Dirt under my nails
And a poetry museum in Piacenza

I'm too tired to stop and say my prayers
Poetry must go on without me

*

Michael Rothenberg

Auschwitz
Belsen

I have no desire to visit these places
Where petals divide like sepulchers

And the religious man rots in a glass coffin
Algae blossoms from his hands

And his corpse white hair rests on a golden pillow
There is no silver mask that can prepare me for this

*

I walk alone
A bell rings through the orange poppies.

May 21, 2014

Bozo the Slick

I will not follow
The plot of a narcissistic madman
Reliving fabricated war stories
In a Napa swimming pool

He sells revolution like Willie Loman

In a shuttle bus from Fiumicino Airport
On my way to Rome Central Train Station

And then to Napoli …

*

A failed script, obsolete play book
Paternalistic name-dropper
Small town opera star with bad teeth

He should give up and go into retirement
Nobody believes in him
Or his phony Hollywood style

At Teatro San Carlos the dilettante is a flop
And what's worse he doesn't
Really believe in change

Michael Rothenberg

He's an opportunist
Who always needs to feel important
A politician that wants to be an onion

      Eventualist, Enabler, Fraud

Every action a salve upon
His failed self

Maybe he's a cop!

      *

Is that the Coliseum or an ancient jumpy house
Managed by a gladiator from Burger Chef?
Is that the Forum or his vanity
Smeared over broken bowels, skinny
Spotted legs stuffed into teenage blue jeans?

It's difficult to grow old with dignity
So he calls the Attorney General
Makes plans for a compromised peace
With the Department of Injustice
Then runs from the plain Truth
When the mirror plays back

His pathetic, lightless regime
Baby Mussolini!

*

I would rather be in Postiglione
Fighting the good fight
With Valeriano, Filippo, and Terri
Espresso in one hand, *zeppela* in the other

The taste so sincere …

*

Alburni,
Virgil, in *Bucoliche*, saw this mountain
Long before the bakery opened downtown

We walk over to the supermarket
Buy some pancetta, cherry tomatoes, ricotta tart
Charcoal to grill fresh sausages
Peach jam for breakfast

*

Michael Rothenberg

Bozo the Slick
He's been nobody his whole life
Tells you what he thinks you want to hear
So you'll purchase his particular brand of laxative
With a knot in his tongue here comes the pitch
Bullshit!

*

In Postiglione

Bill Evans plays in the kitchen
Outside the windows' blue moon
Skies around the rocky peaks
A wine-soaked phantasm
Breaks the code

*

Alburni …
Virgil saw this mountain

There was a thunderstorm pelted
The terra cotta shingles
We shivered through the Amalfi night

In a house built in 700 AD
In a town built long before the redwoods

*

He's a jester in tailored shirts and mod coiffure
What is he saying exactly?
A broken hero who sells courage
Without justice

A cannibal and poser
Who feeds on your dreams
A wolf in sheep's clothing
Who celebrates in collateral damage
A savior on hunt for medals

*

Limoncello
Custard-stuffed croissant

In my heart
I am looking for a cologne that smells like fresh
Baked bread when the loaf is first divided
There's a crunch when you bite down
And the fragrance is one of veracity

Michael Rothenberg

Ten thousand miles from a
Two-faced clown, Postiglione
Salerno, Cava de' Tirreni, Naples, Amalfi, Pompeii
Temple of Venus and Hercules
Everywhere, a thousand other places
Beautiful and true, even in Rome
Far from a doctored and circus fiction.

May 14, 2014

Miracle Pastry

The pastry is a miracle
That's how morning begins

> A geode of deliciousness
> Precious ricotta crystals
> Buttery flakes dusted with powdered sugar

Massive unemployment
Followed by installation of
The Virgin Mary at San Pietro in Bologna

> Come to Italy!

Sure things are bad
Corruption everywhere
We've all suffered defeat
But don't give up
There is always Pasticceria della Rocca

> As bodies fall in Santa Barbara
> Each delicate crumb
>   becomes an epic verse

Put a smiley face on a thug!
Filo Renaissance

Michael Rothenberg

Byzantine Universalism
Ambient horror

The croissant is stuffed with yellow custard
There's grace in culinary expatriation

    Profiterole, cannoli, Neopolitans!

Wipe away *sturm und drang*

    O Sole mio!

I will never be alone with a tart in my bed
The comfort of crumbs in my flesh
While I sleep, toss and turn among crunchy, sweet

    Omens of potentiality

And if I dream of mechanical eagles
With bloody guns for talons
I only need to wake up
And smell the espresso

    There's always time to remember
    The deportations
    Wish upon a revolution

But now the sun shines through my window
And my plate is filled with delicious art.

May 24, 2014
Imola

Michael Rothenberg

No Grandi Navi

Seagulls

           w/ prehistoric wings

                                fly

over the giant cruise ship

                tugged down

                          Canale della Giudecca

              Cathedrals

become Lilliputian chapels

                          dwarfed by

    the cruise ship

                      w/ polyglot, megaphonic

                            voice

            that echoes

and enshrouds

                        history

                                        while we drink

our golden drinks

                 at a cafe

                                  in Giudecca

        We erode

                            w/ each sip of spritz

and vanish

                    in red waves of sunset

as the leisure cruise ship

the surreal cruise ship

the ghostly cruise ship

Michael Rothenberg

      swallows up

           gondolas

              and the shadows

of gondolas

                  The cruise ship

    w/ six thousand souls

                    each w/ their own

    smart phone

                   taking pictures of themselves

      duplicate themselves

    in a floating casino

                 consume themselves

into poverty

        in the oceanic mall

                on the upper deck

     of the cruise ship

in Venice

                The cruise ships

     taller

     wider

                stranger than Venice

follow in procession

                The cruise ships

where tourism is

                an arena sport

     where the crowd

Michael Rothenberg

                                          on all decks

                                                        cheer

to remember the future

                                      witness the spectacle

                of Marco Polo

                                        Lord Byron

and Ezra Pound

                        The cruise ship

                                          the megalithic

cruise ship

                in obliterating glory

                                            floats by.

                                                    May 2014

Wooden Ducks

Your poems are wooden ducks
They don't go anywhere
on their own

Like a seagull on a stick
A soulless mallard
set adrift

Yes, I value your opinion

But your poems are splinters
removed from your ass
after sitting too long
on a bench

Carved and painted decoys

You hide behind the willows
Make those poetry sounds
and when real poems
show up …

    Boom!

May 30, 2014
Giudecca Island

Michael Rothenberg

When I Was in Italy

When I was in Italy I was happy enough
With a ham sandwich and an orange soda

Now it's the day after Labor Day in the USA
Terri's gone to class to learn Italian

And my 23-year-old son
Worries me to death

*

The moon is never full enough
I crawl the raw walls inside my naked skin

Send greetings to imaginary friends
"Goodnight and good morning

Poets of the World!
Peace will come, I know it will," I say

As quietly as a blue jay in the garden
But poets question everything

They're never satisfied
Fair is never fair enough

There must be a solution!

    *

Go away slavery and don't come back
I hate your shadowlands of privilege

You make me ashamed with your
Razor-wire fences

Petty citizenships
Cultural slaughterhouses

Red, white and blue dappled brains

    Sigh …

    *

In the lobby of the County office
Waiting for an appointment

With a member of the Board of Supervisors
I overhear a man and a woman

Michael Rothenberg

Seated beside me talking about
Drought and global warming

They are very concerned
And look to the local weather for solutions

The woman says, "I hate the fog. Well, I
shouldn't say I hate it, I'm challenged by it"

She's challenged by it!
Innocent enough, a linguistic anomaly

I'm sure she's challenged by the long
Soggy gray scale

This country bordered by nagging
Pre-existing conditions of race and color

This fog of convenient exclusion
Forever in pursuit of an immaculate clime

Caucasians confuse me....

*

When I was in Italy I was content
With fava beans and Pecorino Romano

Now it's almost Thanksgiving in the USA
It will be absolutely perfect here

When we flush out this inferior race
Deport the aliens

This perplexing and uncontrollable mist
Send these gloomy dreamers

Back to wherever they came from
Wherever they belong

Racist Patriots patrol the border!

    *

"The best way to stop a bad guy with a gun
    is to take away his badge"

    *

I'm looking for Justice!
Put this Homeland on gang terms

Michael Rothenberg

But first let me fix something that isn't broken
It's time for lunch

Get in that jail cell and I will be right back
I want a ham sandwich on a toasted roll

Slathered with brown mustard
In Italy ...

      *

Now what was I saying?

    Burp!

I am challenged by inequality
But no one said life is fair

I saw myself on the floor one night
Or was that my son alone

In early morning light
Absorbed in trinket memories?

Marksmen medals from camp
A pocket knife

Grandma's keychain kaleidoscope
Granddad's racetrack opera glasses

Paintbrushes
We try to make sense of things

Pieces of things, connect the dots
Extrapolate but

        as long as you are in the way
    with your indifferences

I'm going to have to go look
For a private school

"I'm at work. I'll call you later," my son says
But he never calls and I don't think he works

He says I'm a race traitor
For marrying a Mexican

Even though she's Cuban
From the white part of Spain

It's a challenge
No matter where or who you are

Michael Rothenberg

Or on which side of the inversion
You think is yours

It's not Italy, this ham sandwich
It's tuna fish. This factoried perfection

This conditional applause
But it will have to do

        Apartheid in California!

    *

I am challenged
By the red roses that flourish

Beyond a cultivated indifference
On the other side of the border fence

The promise of fog and that sandwich
I will never get to eat again.

November 9, 2014

The Portal

As if each leaf

        and stone that fell

        condemned

              a universe

Some star or body

      pierced by choral gravity

          resumes its outward journey

          Strains

              against arterial buckles and cuffs

Strewn across the night

Vegetal clacking and boom

        Saw-grass plains

        Orange restless swale

Michael Rothenberg

        Heave and rust

                in the portal eye

        Tsunami

A palm-frond boat

    Dewy chameleons blush and puff

           in mute and corrugated antiphony

Slider, strangler, skimmer

Sunrise through tilted blinds

Anabolic latitudes

Blossoms exhumed

        On the angry brink

In the ragged wake of tropical alleys.

                      December 17, 2014

Wake Up and Dream

1. *Moderate Rebel*

Seated on the doorstep with a suitcase and nowhere to go
The world around me falls away
Invisible day becomes eternal
I am floating
A planet caught in an intangible orbit nowhere I know
A figment of gravity's imagination set adrift.

Michael Rothenberg

2. The Fate of Nations

They might as well be dogs barking on the street
Vendors in the market
An opera of squid, oranges, and peppered olives
The fate of nations in an extinct dialogue,
reciting poems, conspiring a revolution of conscience,
headlining the daily chronicle

They might as well be mercenary soldiers
who occupy the epic shrines and holy ruins
For who could imagine the naked butchers
and their brides in armor?

3. *The Madonnas*

On Monday we will be moving those ghosts
and monoliths into the church

The shattered Madonnas will be kept in storage.

Michael Rothenberg

4. There Will Be Slaves

There will be queens, presidents, laureates and slaves
Cicada and a calamity of brass bells in a chorus
at 2 a.m., when the shadows stretch and bend
across the heavy doors of the spirit swollen church

Poets from Paris, Sacramento and Kuala Lumpur
will begin a serenade, take on a puppet Broadway,
a stoned choreography in the piazza,
while children in pajamas crawl out on moonlit balconies,
watch through curtains of night-drying laundry,
dripping blouses and large pink underwear,
the dance and fermentation of the spoken word....

There will be a quake, a mutant rhyme, a seagull cry
Then change will come

A breeze from the broad blue Tyrrhenian Sea
The resurrection of green with every lava-buried breath,
disabling cobble and utopian *abbracci*

It will come
The change

And then the children will go back to bed
The police will never say a word
The clock will unwind and all the poets of the world
will march in celebration of another broken law
Another pantomime of insurrection.

5. Palmyra

Each footstool
Ballerina
Banana peel
Sweet cheese

Each corrugated brain fissure
Divinity side street
Poetry

Each gun
Incarceration
Cantaloupe, honeysuckle hedge

Each rotation, sock, shirt, pair of shorts
on the rusty balcony

Each marble discus thrower
etched in nocturnal frost
on Dr. Caligari's China cabinet

Each immigrant boat that sinks
Palmyra has fallen.

6. Waiting to Happen

O sweet buoyant orb!
My fair-born child!

I miss you
I love you
I hate you
I want you

Sucking up to that easy prize
Sure you can have it both ways, if you want
The gold-plated ring and eternal stars
but never disembowel the cool alley cat
on its randy way home
to a dish of warm milk and grappa
in the solitary swing
of a black and silver accordion serenade
because there's a real poem in that

She walks cobbled streets on crutches....

I miss you
I love you
I hate you
I want you

Michael Rothenberg

"I want to be together (somewhere else)," she says
You're breaking my heart, Salerno....

Pasticcerria!

La Dolce Vita

Up again, down again
All across town
While she's stuck in an elevator
between process and anarchy
It's a spidery dance on a red full moon
Bagpipe and tambourine
Tomatoes and castanets
Blue, yellow, and orange paper poetry boats
float in the fountain at Piazza Abate Conforti

"Let our dreams come true," they say

O, buffalo mozzarella!
Bathed in seaweed and sand

"I want to be together (somewhere else)."

7. When All The Beautiful Souls Arrive

Seagull perched on the terra cotta roof
Flame skimmer dragonfly in poetry's spirit
All blue jays and pilgrims and fellow travelers
Looking further than the full red moon.

Michael Rothenberg

8. *Drunk on a Thousand Willows*

Dead mice and pine needles in the garbage heap
It could have been something beautiful
Brutal and silent

Those wheelbarrows turned upside down
The mop in the bucket by the woodpile
The contradictory gift of twin valleys

Two steps forward, ten steps back
Fresh water mostly runs through the pipes
Occasionally the pipes break
So I tear the wall down, repair the leak
Replace the wall and move on

Like a battering ram through love.

9. The Imaginary Window

Remember when a handshake meant something
(Feeling nostalgic)
And oranges were sunshine or an immortal poem
Outside was outside and not another
inside never considered?

Just because he has long hair doesn't make him liberal
Just because he's Jewish doesn't mean he's like me
That's what my mother told me when we took the television
to be repaired on Normandy Isle a half-century ago

"You can't trust anyone," she said
There is no way to build a tribe
Beat, subtle light and trust in a slant House of Mirrors
(My, you're looking tall today! Or short today)

Shaped by time
The shape of time
We stand alone before a crushing glacier
Melt with the continent
Flow in the dark
A vanishing star
A sound never heard in the universe.

Michael Rothenberg

10. The Ride

I am waiting now for the perfect storm to course the rails
A current to eclipse resistance and lift me up above the clouds

Almanacs and headlines foretell a troubled magnificence
For better or worse, I will soon be going
on my sun-drenched way

Mosquitoes sing around my ears, bite my ankles and neck
A thousand blue words spill and lacerate an ivory birth

Some say there will be no peace
until everyone is rich and famous
So we cross another border to bury a child in the sand

Where do we come from, so many of us,
our backs against the sea?
Refugees, the price we pay for dropping bombs

Let's go, again, down again, on again and stop
Here is the family. A little girl wails in her grandma's arms

Her mother and father drowned on the bloody travail
The price she pays for hunger, dreams and abstractions

Yes, let's go, she says, never looking back. *Here comes the ride Together we will run. I am a dreamer like you.*

September 8, 2015

Michael Rothenberg

11. *Wake Up and Dream*

The eye floats across a ringing silence
A snow-blind underworld descent
One snap comes from heat as the light dies
Another as the burden of the world impales the night

Maple leaves flash and flicker in a twilight gust
The manifestation of an invisible genocide
Rout and blood of an impossible enemy
The course of an accidental universe
An unrelenting gourd on fire

The eye continues its liquid journey
across the chemical mind
A synaptical rhetoric seizes the translucent promise,
swells and shreds until fictive rainbows,
the black silk petals of a premature resurrection
and the late-blossoming shadows of a sinking harmony,
mutter through our morning prayers:

"Wake up and dream, wake up and dream…."

Acknowledgments

Early drafts of "The Portal" first appeared in "Stone Renga Poem." In 2015, "Serenity Spring" and "Revolt of the Donkeys" were published in *Nuova antologia di poesia americana*, Ediz. Multilingue, translated by Alessandra Bava. "The Blue Jays" appeared in *Cape Cod Poetry Review* and *Of Nepalese Clay* (Kathmandu, Nepal); "When I Was in Italy" appeared in *The Border Crossed Us* (an anthology to end apartheid), published by Vagabond (2015); "Skinhead" in *Sensitive Skin Magazine*; "Revolt of the Donkeys" and "Remembering *The Majoon Traveler*" in *Truck*; "You're Broke, On Drugs and Monsanto Owns You," "Platform 18 Milano Centrale" and "Independence Day" in *Dispatches from The Poetry Wars*; "The March" appeared in *Golden Handcuffs* (2017); "Terroristic" in *LiVE MAG!* (2015); "*Plus C'est La Même Chose* Agadir" in *HOWL* (Humanities Opposition World League); "Bozo the Slick" in *Journal of Poetics Research*; and "Wake Up and Dream" first appeared in *Local Knowledge*.

About the Author

MICHAEL ROTHENBERG is a poet, editor and publisher of the online literary magazine BigBridge.org, co-founder of 100 Thousand Poets for Change (100tpc.org), and co-founder of Poets In Need, a non-profit 501(c)(3), assisting poets in crisis. Born in Miami Beach, Florida in 1951, Rothenberg moved to the San Francisco Bay Area in 1975 and co-founded Shelldance Orchid Gardens in Pacifica, which is dedicated to the cultivation of orchids and bromeliads. While in Pacifica, he helped lead local environmental actions that stopped major coastal developments that would destroy wildlife habitat.

He has published 20 books of poetry, including *Nightmare of The Violins, Favorite Songs, Man/Women* (a collaboration with Joanne Kyger), *Unhurried Vision, Monk Daddy, The Paris Journals, Choose, My Youth As A Train,* and *Murder.* His most recent books of poetry include *Sapodilla* (Editions du Cygne-Swan World, Paris, France, 2016) and *Drawing The Shade* (Dos Madres Press, 2016). Bilingual editions of *Indefinite Detention: A Dog Story*, and the collection of poetic journals *Tally Ho and The Cowboy Dream/The Real and False Journals: Book 5* is due out from Varasek Ediciones, Madrid, Spain, in fall 2017.

His work has been published widely in literary reviews and included in anthologies such as *Ecopoetry: A Contemporary American Anthology*, edited by Ann Fisher-Wirth and Laura-Gray Street (Trinity University Press), *43 Poetas por Ayotzinapa*, edited by Jesús González Alcántara and Moisés H. Cortés Cruz (Mexico), *Saints of Hysteria, A Half-Century of Collaborative American Poetry*, edited by David Trinidad and Denise Duhamel (Soft Skull Press), *Hidden Agendas/Unreported Poetics*, edited by Louis Armand (Litteraria Pragensia), and *For the Time-Being: The Bootstrap Book of Poetic Journals*, edited by Tyler Doherty and Tom Morgan (Bootstrap Productions).

Michael Rothenberg

Rothenberg's editorial work includes several volumes in the Penguin Poets series: *Overtime* by Philip Whalen, *As Ever* by Joanne Kyger, *David's Copy* by David Meltzer, and *Way More West* by Edward Dorn. Rothenberg is also editor of *The Collected Poems of Philip Whalen* published by Wesleyan University Press (2007). In 2016, Rothenberg moved back to Florida. He currently lives on Lake Jackson in Tallahassee, Florida, with his partner Terri Carrion and their two dogs, Ziggy and Puma.

www.ingramcontent.com/pod-product-compliance
Lightning Source LLC
Chambersburg PA
CBHW020336170426
43200CB00006B/412

Praise for *Wake Up and Dream*

The current dangerous political moment did not arrive all at once, though for many in the U.S. it seemed so. Others had been watching for a long time, reporting directly from the home grounds of injustice, inequality, and despair. As *Wake Up and Dream* makes clear, Michael Rothenberg has been one of those prescient witnesses to intransigent problems that history has not been able to sweep away. Often the poems collected here express outrage at eruptions of cruelty, as they should. Often they register with dismay events in which people (literally) got away with murder. The poet is angry—as am I. And yet, truth be told, these poems are suffused not with anger but with love. And, ultimately, love is the truth they tell and hold. Read this book, aloud; read this book in silence, to yourself; read this book again, with love.

—*Lyn Hejinian*

"Wake Up and Dream"—so Michael Rothenberg enjoins us in this winning book. In a dangerous time, we can look to this poet for solace, humor, and good sense.

—*Aram Saroyan*

Michael Rothenberg is an acrobat of the drastic mood swing, from the self-doubter's Gethsemane to the elevated cross of the Universal Redeemer. The marvel is that his poetry, at both extremes and every point in between, maintains a perfect consistency of clarity, wisdom and wit.

—*Tom Bradley*

Michael Rothenberg's poetry observes & rages, loves & despairs, gets tender, gets resigned, deals with all the emotive intermittence musically, makes big buzzing soundscapes of protest & short lyrics of dignified beauty have equal space, and looks to explore the world rather than reduce it to bites of judgment. The poems in his *Wake Up and Dream* strike me as written, imagined, lived, and built all at once, in time & on a remarkably human scale. They're steeped in the emotional range and depth of an experienced consciousness working hard and long in that zone where the so-called practicality of linear representation runs into the impractical necessity of resisting that narrow take on reality by exploding it, visibly and invisibly, with ferocity and kindness."

—*Anselm Berrigan*